American Principles of Freedom

A Latter-day Saint Perspective

By
Larry Richman

CENTURY PUBLISHING

SALT LAKE CITY, UTAH

American Principles of Freedom: A Latter-day Saint Perspective, by Larry Richman

ISBN 978-0-941846-45-5

centurypubl.com

info@centurypubl.com

This book was written in celebration of America's 250th anniversary. It is not affiliated with, nor endorsed by, the United States Semiquincentennial Commission or America250.org.

Proudly printed in the United States of America.

Contents

Introduction

This book is written in celebration of the 250th anniversary of America's founding. It is written for the rising generation who will become the next stewards of faith, freedom, and responsibility in this nation. Its purpose is to help you understand the values that shaped the United States of America and how these values connect with restored gospel teachings. It will help you learn the principles that created a free and prosperous nation.

The story of America is not only political. It is also spiritual. Latter-day Saint scripture teaches that God prepared this land so freedom could grow and the gospel could be restored. In the Book of Mormon, the Lord teaches that you are free to choose liberty and eternal life or captivity and misery.[1] Modern prophets[2] and latter-day scriptures[3] testify that the Constitution was inspired by God. The founding of America was part of His plan,

---

[1] 2 Nephi 2:27

[2] See "Defending Our Divinely Inspired Constitution," by Dallin H. Oaks, April 2021 General Conference; "The Constitution—A Glorious Standard," by Ezra Taft Benson, April 1976 General Conference; "Civic Standards for the Faithful Saints," by Ezra Taft Benson, April 1972 General Conference; and "The Proper Role of Government," by Ezra Taft Benson.

[3] See Doctrine and Covenants 101:77, 80; 109:54; 98:5–6. Doctrine and Covenants 134 is a declaration of belief regarding governments and laws in general.

and agency, responsibility, and righteous choices are essential to that plan.

America's founding leaders knew they were creating something new in the world. They debated seriously but shared the belief that their work would shape the future of self-government. They taught that the nation would rise or fall on the virtue and courage of its people. They believed that individual rights come from God and that government should be designed to protect those rights. These beliefs shaped the Declaration of Independence, the Constitution, and the work that followed.

Personal responsibility matters because agency is sacred.[4] Limited government is needed because people must be able to guide their own lives. Strong families and good values often protect freedom more effectively than government programs. When families teach honesty, responsibility, and respect, society becomes safer and more stable.

How to Use This Book

This book will guide you through a simple timeline of the American founding. You will learn about the key documents that shape our government and protect freedom. You will study basic principles that guide our freedoms and see how these principles fit with gospel teachings about agency, moral living, and the sacred role of the family.

---

[4] See 2 Nephi 10:23, Doctrine and Covenants 101:78, and Moses 4:3.

My invitation to you is simple. Consider how the principles in this book might bless your life. The American founders showed courage in creating a nation based on freedom and virtue. Courage is needed again today, and you can be part of that work. You can defend freedom by living righteously, strengthening your family, speaking truth with kindness, and choosing to act rather than be acted upon.[5]

May this book help you understand your heritage, love your country, and honor your faith. Freedom survives only when it is valued, protected, and passed to each new generation.

---

[5] 2 Nephi 2:26

CHAPTER 1

The Story of the American Founding

To understand the American founding, it helps to understand the world that led to it. The founding did not appear suddenly. It developed over many centuries as people learned about responsibility, faith, law, and the worth of every person. They learned that liberty is freedom that is organized and protected by law so that everyone's rights can coexist. The founders of the Constitution were wise men raised up by God.[6] They saw themselves as part of a long story in which people grew in experience and learned how to govern themselves with wisdom.

The brief timeline that follows shows the events, ideas, and influences that prepared the way for the United States of America. It highlights the culture, conflicts, and principles that helped shape the American mind.

Early Foundations in English History

Magna Carta (1215)

Centuries before the American founding, English nobles challenged the king's unlimited power. The Magna Carta

---

[6] Doctrine and Covenants 101:80.

placed limits on the monarchy and declared that leaders must obey the law. It introduced the idea that no one is above the law and that people deserve basic protections.

Developing Traditions of Rights and Representation

Over time, England developed institutions like Parliament, trial by jury, and protection of property. These became known as the ancient rights of Englishmen. They taught that government should serve the people, not rule over them. The American founders respected these rights and believed they were defending them during the Revolution.

The Pilgrims, Puritans, and the Quest for Religious Liberty

In the 1600s many settlers came to America to escape the control of kings and churches who demanded that people live and worship as they said, rather than let them be free to make their own choices. The Mayflower Compact set an early pattern for self-government. Families agreed to work together and live by common rules. This simple agreement helped build the American tradition of responsibility and community cooperation.

These early settlements, or colonies, also showed that virtue, family, and faith play an important role in building a free society.

Growth of the Colonies and Emerging American Identity

As the colonies expanded through the 1600s and 1700s, people gained experience in self-government. They elected local leaders, debated issues, and managed community affairs. These experiences gave colonists confidence that they could guide their own lives.

By the mid-1700s the people in the colonies saw themselves not only as British citizens but also as a people with their own identity and expectations of liberty. They wanted the right to own property, run their own businesses, and live in a society where everyone obeyed the law.

Rising Tensions with Great Britain

Taxation and Representation

After the French and Indian War, Great Britain taxed the colonies to pay war costs. Laws like the Stamp Act and Townshend Acts angered colonists who believed taxes should come only from their own elected assemblies.

Boston Tea Party (1773)

When Britain passed the Tea Act, colonists protested by dumping tea into Boston Harbor. Their action was both a protest and a statement of principle. They believed they should not be ruled without their consent.

The Coercive Acts

Britain responded with harsh measures that closed Boston's port and weakened colonial self-rule. These actions convinced many colonists that their rights were at risk.

Americans believed they were defending long-standing principles of freedom, not creating new ones. They felt they were protecting the rights they had always held.

First Continental Congress (1774)

Delegates from the colonies met to decide how to respond to British oppression. They created the Articles of Association, which organized a shared effort to resist unjust laws. They also stressed unity and mutual support. This showed the growing belief that free people must stand together when their rights are in danger.

The Road to Revolution (1775)

Battles of Lexington and Concord

British troops tried to seize colonial weapons, and local militia resisted. These first battles showed that many Americans were ready to defend their rights and freedoms.

Second Continental Congress

The Second Continental Congress organized military efforts and began discussing independence. George Washington was chosen to lead the Continental Army. His strong character and sense of duty gave the nation confidence during this uncertain time.

Declaration of Independence (1776)

After many efforts to settle disagreements peacefully, the colonies chose independence. The Declaration of Independence taught several eternal truths. It taught that rights come from God, that government exists to protect those rights, and that people can change a government that violates those rights.

These principles show how freedom works in everyday life. You should use your agency wisely, take responsibility for your actions, and make choices that lead to a better life.

The Revolutionary War (1775–1783)

The Revolutionary War was long and difficult. Key victories at Trenton, Saratoga, and Yorktown gave the Americans hope and strengthened the American resolve. The founders endured many hardships because they believed they were defending sacred trust and helping create a nation where freedom could last.

Articles of Confederation (1781)

The Articles of Confederation created a loose union of states with very limited national power. This system helped the states work together during the war, but it soon showed its weaknesses. The new nation needed a stronger government to solve shared problems, settle disputes, and protect the general welfare. The founders learned through experience that freedom must be protected by law so that everyone's rights can coexist.

The Constitutional Convention (1787)

Delegates met in Philadelphia to create a stronger and more effective national government. Their debates were serious, but they shared the same basic goals. They wanted to protect liberty, prevent abuses of power, establish order, and preserve self-government.

The Constitution they created set up a system with separated powers and checks and balances that has guided the nation ever since. The delegates understood that they were shaping the future of freedom and felt a deep responsibility for the work they were doing.

Ratification, the Federalist Papers, and the Bill of Rights (1787–1791)

The states held long debates about the new Constitution. Writers such as James Madison, Alexander Hamilton, and John Jay explained its purpose in the Federalist Papers. The Bill of Rights was added soon after to protect freedoms like speech, religion, and property. These protections showed that the founders valued the dignity of every person and expected leaders to act with honesty and responsibility.

The New Nation Begins (1789–1800)

When George Washington became the first President, the United States began to put its new government into practice. Early leaders set important examples, strengthened national unity, and showed how free institutions should work.

The period concluded with a peaceful transfer of power in 1800, proving that self-government based on strong principles could succeed.

Why This Timeline Matters

The American Founding was more than a series of events. It was shaped by ideas about human worth, personal responsibility, faith, strong families, and the limits of government. The founders taught that every generation must live these principles with care. They knew that freedom does not last by itself. It requires virtue, wisdom, and the courage to choose what is right.

This timeline shows that the United States grew out of lasting truths. These truths form the foundation of the values and principles that continue to bless free people today.

CHAPTER 2

Biographies of Key Founders of America

The founding of America was shaped by remarkable individuals who combined courage, wisdom, sacrifice, and dedication to fundamental principles. Below are short biographies of a few of the most influential people, describing their character, their ideas, and the roles they played in creating a nation built on liberty.

George Washington

George Washington was born in Virginia in 1732 and became the central leader of the founding generation. He commanded the Continental Army and helped the colonies survive the hardships of the Revolutionary War. After the war, he presided over the Constitutional Convention and later became the first President of the United States.

Washington inspired trust because of his humility, duty, and moral strength. He willingly gave up power when his service was complete. His leadership set the pattern for future presidents and helped the young nation begin on a foundation of virtue and self-control. Washington also helped unite a people with very different backgrounds and encouraged Americans to put the good of the country above personal interest.

Benjamin Franklin

Benjamin Franklin was born in Boston in 1706 and became one of the most remarkable thinkers of the eighteenth century. He was a scientist, inventor, diplomat, publisher, and writer. He helped draft the Declaration of Independence, represented the colonies in France, and served as a key voice at the Constitutional Convention.

Franklin's practical wisdom and love of learning shaped American civic life. He believed a free society needed virtue, hard work, and common sense. He also encouraged personal improvement through habits such as daily reflection and honest living. Franklin's inventions, public projects, and efforts to strengthen community life showed his belief that citizens should use their talents to bless others.

John Adams

John Adams was born in Massachusetts in 1735 and became one of the strongest voices for American independence. He helped draft the Declaration of Independence and later served as the first Vice President and the second President of the United States.

Adams was known for his honesty, sense of duty, and belief in obeying the law. He taught that government depends on moral citizens and that freedom requires virtue. He also urged Americans to value education and to build strong institutions that would protect liberty. Adams defended the rights of the accused even when it was unpopular, showing his commitment to justice and principle.

Thomas Jefferson

Thomas Jefferson was born in Virginia in 1743 and is best known as the main author of the Declaration of Independence. He served as Governor of Virginia, diplomat to France, Secretary of State, Vice President, and President of the United States. He helped guide the early nation through major decisions and supported the growth of peaceful political change.

Jefferson was a strong defender of liberty. He believed in natural rights, religious freedom, and the need for people to be educated. Although he held complex views and personal contradictions, his ideas about equality and human dignity still influence American life. Jefferson also advanced learning by founding the University of Virginia, which reflected his belief that education strengthens both citizens and the nation.

James Madison

James Madison was born in Virginia in 1751 and is known as the Father of the Constitution. He played a leading role in shaping the structure of the new government at the Constitutional Convention and wrote many of the Federalist Papers. He later served as Secretary of State and as President of the United States.

Madison had a remarkable understanding of both human nature and political theory. He taught that freedom requires both virtue and carefully balanced institutions. He knew that no single person or group should have the power to control everything. Therefore, he proposed the idea of "separation of powers" and "checks and balances." These ideas are central to American government. Madison also helped guide the Bill of Rights through Congress, showing his belief that liberty must be protected by clear and lasting safeguards.

Alexander Hamilton

Alexander Hamilton was born in the West Indies in either 1755 or 1757 and rose from humble beginnings to become a key architect of the new nation. He served as an aide to General Washington during the Revolutionary War, coauthored the Federalist Papers, and became the first Secretary of the Treasury.

Hamilton worked to build a strong and stable economy. He helped create the nation's financial system and promoted national unity. He believed that a strong but limited national government could support prosperity and keep the country secure. Hamilton also helped organize the nation's first bank and encouraged growth in trade and industry, shaping the future economic direction of the United States.

Patrick Henry

Patrick Henry was born in Virginia in 1736 and became famous for his powerful speeches, including his declaration, "Give me liberty or give me death." He was a strong defender of the rights of the colonies and later of the states.

Henry valued personal liberty and local self-government. He feared that a strong central government might take away the freedoms that Americans had fought for. Although he opposed the Constitution at first, his concerns helped inspire the creation of the Bill of Rights.

Henry also encouraged ordinary citizens to stay involved in public life and to speak boldly for their principles.

Thomas Paine

Thomas Paine was born in England in 1737 and came to America shortly before the Revolution. His famous pamphlet *Common Sense* helped unite the colonies and build strong support for independence. He later wrote about government, individual rights, and the dignity of every person.

Paine was a powerful writer who explained complex ideas in simple language that ordinary people could understand. His passion for liberty strengthened public resolve during the Revolution and helped many Americans see their struggle as part of a worldwide desire for freedom. Paine also wrote *The American Crisis,* which inspired soldiers and citizens during some of the most difficult moments of the war.

CHAPTER 3

Why the Founding of America Matters

The founding of the United States matters because it became a major turning point in history. For the first time, a nation was built on the idea that people could govern themselves through reason, virtue, and cooperation rather than through force or inherited power. The founders believed that ordinary people, when guided by moral character and true principles, could build a free and successful society. Their work introduced a new way of thinking about government and the worth of every person.

The founders knew they were part of something extraordinary. They understood that if their experiment in self-government succeeded, it would show the world that people can rise above fear and oppression and live by reason, justice, and equality. They also understood that if they failed, many might claim that freedom is unsafe and that people cannot govern themselves. The founders felt a deep responsibility to show that liberty is possible when it is protected by law and when people obey those laws so that everyone's rights can coexist.

The founding matters because it taught important and lasting truths about human nature. It showed that all people are equal in worth and dignity. It taught that rights come from God rather than from kings or governments, and that governments are created to protect those rights. These ideas helped change the world. They gave hope to people who believed in agency and responsibility. They also provided a clear standard for citizens and leaders to judge their actions.

The founding matters because Latter-day Saints believe that God inspired the Constitution to protect the freedom to choose. Moral agency, the power to decide and act, is an important reason God sent us to earth. We use this gift best when we have the freedom to act according to our choices.[7]

The founding matters because it created a government built on structure, balance, and accountability. The Constitution set up a system that directs human ambition through laws and institutions. The founders knew that people can do great good but can also act selfishly. They created a government strong enough to keep peace and order yet limited enough to prevent any one person or group from controlling everything. They taught that freedom is safest when power is divided and no person or group controls the whole system. Their design protects liberty for future generations.

The founding also matters because it confirmed the need for virtue in public life. The founders often taught that political freedom depends on private morality. Citizens

---

[7] See Doctrine and Covenants 101:77, 80; 109:54; 98:5–6; 134:5; and "Defending Our Divinely Inspired Constitution," by President Dallin H. Oaks, April 2021 General Conference.

must learn self-control so they can govern themselves wisely. Leaders must act with integrity so that people can trust their institutions. Families must teach honesty, hard work, and respect. These values help a free society to function. When citizens or leaders fail to live these principles, the system struggles, not because the system is flawed, but because people are imperfect. The founders knew their work would last only if future generations remained committed to duty, sacrifice, and moral character.

Another reason the founding matters is that it helped create a nation open to many kinds of people. America had no ancient monarchy, no single tribe, and no ruling class. It was built on universal principles that apply to all people in every place. The founders taught that every person has God given rights, regardless of background or social class. This made America different from every nation before it.

Because of these ideas, people could unite around shared principles rather than bloodlines or social status. America became a nation defined by purpose rather than ancestry, which opened the door to millions who came seeking freedom.

The founding also matters to Latter-day Saints because it prepared the way for the Restoration of the gospel. Latter-day scriptures teach that God inspired the Constitution so people could enjoy freedom of conscience.[8] This freedom made it possible for The

---

[8] Doctrine and Covenants 101:80, 101:77, 109:54, 98:5–6, and 134:5.

Church of Jesus Christ of Latter-day Saints to be organized and to grow. Ideas about agency, accountability, and moral choice appear both in the founding documents and in the teachings of the restored gospel. The founding created a safe place where truth could return and spread throughout the world.

Finally, the founding matters because its work is continuing. Every generation must renew its commitment to the principles that shaped the nation. The founders knew that Americans would need to preserve liberty by living with gratitude, courage, and responsibility. Freedom does not maintain itself automatically. It depends on the character of the people, the strength of families, and the willingness of citizens to defend what is right. The government institutions created at the founding only work when the people use them wisely.

In simple terms, the American founding matters because it showed the world that people can live free when they honor truth and virtue. It created a nation built on God-given rights, the importance of following laws, and personal responsibility. It offered hope to people everywhere and established the foundation for our basic values today. The founding still invites us to live worthy of the blessings we have received.

CHAPTER 4

Basic Documents of the American Founding

The American founding is based on several key documents that express the core values and guiding principles of the new nation. They help explain why the United States developed as it did. These writings explain what the founders believed about human nature, personal liberty, responsibility, and the proper role of government. Each document adds a different part to the story. When you study them together, you begin to see the foundation of American political thought and the ideas that continue to shape our country today.

Articles of Association (1774)

The Articles of Association were adopted by the First Continental Congress as the colonies faced increasing pressure from Great Britain. This agreement united the colonies in a peaceful plan to oppose unjust laws. It encouraged cooperation, responsibility, and self-discipline. It also marked the beginning of a united American identity, built on the belief that free people can work together to protect their rights.

Declaration of Independence (1776)

The Declaration of Independence announced that the colonies were separating from Great Britain. More importantly, it expressed lasting truths about people and their rights. It taught that rights come from God, that governments exist to protect those rights, and that citizens are responsible for choosing leaders and correcting governments that fail to protect those rights.

The Declaration presents a strong vision of human dignity and equal worth. It shows that liberty is a sacred trust and is not given by rulers. This document stands at the foundation of the American story and continues to influence how many Americans understand freedom.

Articles of Confederation (1781)

The Articles of Confederation were a framework for the first national government after independence. They created a partnership among the states but gave very little power to the national government. This reflected the fear of strong central authority and the desire to protect local control. However, the Articles were too weak to handle national problems such as defense, trade, and financial stability. The founders soon learned that liberty needs both freedom and a structure strong enough to support it.

Constitution of the United States (1787)

The Constitution replaced the Articles of Confederation and created a stronger but limited national government. It set up three branches of government, each with clear responsibilities, and balanced power between the federal government and the states. It was designed to protect liberty by establishing clear laws and a system of checks and balances.

The United States Constitution is the oldest written constitution still in effect today. It teaches important principles such as separation of powers, limited government, accountability to the people, and the protection of individual rights. The founders crafted it to secure freedom while preventing any one person or group from controlling everything. Latter-day prophets[9] and latter-day scriptures[10] teach that the Constitution was inspired by God and intended to help protect the freedom to act and choose.

The Bill of Rights

The first ten amendments, known as the Bill of Rights, were added soon after the Constitution was ratified to protect essential freedoms. These include freedom of religion and speech, the right to assemble, protection from unreasonable searches, the right to fair trials, and limits on government power.

---

[9] See "Defending Our Divinely Inspired Constitution," by Dallin H. Oaks, April 2021 General Conference; "The Constitution—A Glorious Standard," by Ezra Taft Benson, April 1976 General Conference; "Civic Standards for the Faithful Saints," by Ezra Taft Benson, April 1972 General Conference; and "The Proper Role of Government," by Ezra Taft Benson.

[10] See Doctrine and Covenants 101:77, 80; 109:54; and 98:5–6. Doctrine and Covenants 134 is a declaration of belief regarding governments and laws in general.

The Bill of Rights reminds us that certain liberties belong to the people and must never be taken away by government.

The Federalist Papers (1787–1788)

The Federalist Papers were essays written by James Madison, Alexander Hamilton, and John Jay to help Americans understand the new Constitution. These essays explain how the Constitution protects liberty by dividing power and encouraging cooperation among the branches of government in practical and meaningful ways.

Two essays became especially important.

- *Federalist No. 10* teaches that people naturally form groups with different interests. A large republic helps prevent any one group from gaining too much power because many voices must be heard.
- *Federalist No. 51* teaches that since people are not perfect, government power must be limited and separated. Each branch must be able to check the others, so no branch or leader becomes too powerful.

Why These Documents Matter

These documents share important themes. They teach that freedom requires responsibility and that rights come from God and must be protected by good laws. They show that the founders valued the dignity of every person and expected leaders to act with honesty and responsibility so that rights would remain secure. They show the importance of virtue, cooperation, and self-government. They are not just historical writings. They help you understand how to keep a society strong, fair, and rooted in good values. They also show how people can work together to protect freedom and treat others with dignity in daily life.

CHAPTER 5

Principles That Protect Freedom

The United States of America was founded on basic principles that shape every part of our nation. These ideas guided the founders as they wrote the Declaration of Independence, the Constitution, and the Bill of Rights. They also influenced their understanding of human nature, virtue, and the proper role of government. They knew that liberty survives best when freedoms are organized and protected by laws so that everyone's rights can coexist.

America's founders believed that a free nation should be built on unchanging truths rather than on temporary preferences or shifting political trends. They saw these principles as a foundation for lasting liberty and for the dignity of every person. These truths remind us that freedom is both a gift and a responsibility that must be used wisely.

These basic principles were not invented in a single moment. They were drawn from centuries of experience, moral insight, and thoughtful debate. The founders believed these principles were essential for any society that wanted to defend liberty, protect human dignity, and encourage strong families and responsible citizenship.

These basic American principles continue to guide the nation today. They express truths about human nature, the purpose of government, and the responsibilities of free people.

Why These Principles Matter

These principles are simple but powerful, and they help people live together in peace. They protect human dignity and encourage personal responsibility. They support strong families and strong communities. They guide leaders toward fairness and humility. They also reflect truths taught in the restored gospel about agency, accountability, and moral living.

By understanding and living these principles, you can help preserve the blessings of liberty that the founders worked so hard to secure.

Government By the People

Before the Constitution, many nations assumed that government power came from kings or from military force. The Constitution taught a new truth. Power comes from the people. America is a constitutional republic where citizens choose representatives to act for them.[11]

Leaders serve only with the people's consent. If government becomes unjust, citizens have the right and

---

[11] "Defending Our Divinely Inspired Constitution," by President Dallin H. Oaks, April 2021 General Conference. See section II.

duty to correct it. This protects freedom and invites everyone to take part in community life.

Consent and agency are important gospel principles. People should direct their own lives and not be ruled by those who claim authority without permission. In America, leaders govern with the consent of the people, which sets this nation apart.

Why This Matters

This principle protects your freedom. It reminds you that your vote, your voice, and your service all matter. When people stay informed and involved, leaders stay accountable and liberty endures.

Rights Come from God

The Declaration of Independence teaches that rights come from God. Government does not give rights. It protects them. The founders built our nation on the eternal truth that every person has God-given rights.

Why This Matters

If rights come from God, then no ruler or majority can rightfully take them away. This keeps your freedom safe even when times are hard or opinions change.

Equality Under God

The Declaration of Independence teaches that all people are created equal and have equal rights. This means that each person has the same moral worth and should receive equal protection under the law. It does not mean that everyone has the same talents or circumstances or that all people will have the same outcomes.

This truth pushed back against the old idea that some people were born to rule. It placed the worth of every person at the center of government and invited humility, compassion, and respect for others.

Why This Matters

Equal worth demands equal treatment. It calls you to see others as God sees them and to support laws that protect everyone's rights.

Universal Moral Truths

Our Constitution is built on the belief that there are universal moral truths that apply to all people. These truths do not come from government, but from God. The founders called this natural law. Natural law teaches that:

- All people are equal in worth, and they should receive equal protection and dignity.
- All people possess equal basic rights.
- These rights do not depend on wealth, race, class, or government approval.
- Governments exist to protect these rights, not to create them.

Natural law sets a clear standard for justice. It reminds citizens and leaders that laws should reflect moral truth. When a government violates natural rights, the people must correct it.

Why This Matters

A shared moral standard helps makes freedom possible. It protects the weak, restrains the strong, and helps communities agree on what is fair.

Rule of Law

Rule of law means that the law applies equally to everyone. Leaders follow the same laws as citizens. No one gets special treatment. This protects people from the abuse of power and guards everyone, regardless of race, gender, social class, or other characteristics.

Freedom lasts only when laws are fair and clear. Rule of law builds trust, keeps order, and preserves justice.

Why This Matters

Rule of law protects you from unfair treatment. It keeps powerful people accountable and gives everyone confidence that justice will be done.

Due Process

Due process requires the government to act fairly before it takes life, liberty, or property. It includes the right to know the charges against you, the right to defend yourself with evidence, and the right to a fair and impartial trial. Due process guards the innocent and keeps justice careful rather than rushed.

Why This Matters

Due process protects you from wrongful punishment. It keeps courts fair and limits government power in your daily life.

Habeas Corpus

Habeas corpus is a legal protection that prevents people from being imprisoned without a clear and lawful reason. It allows anyone who is detained to ask a court to review the case and decide whether the detention is lawful. This principle has protected freedom for centuries. It stops governments from holding people secretly or indefinitely and ensures that no person loses liberty without justification.

Why This Matters

Habeas corpus protects you from wrongful or unfair imprisonment. It ensures that no one, including the government, can take away your freedom without approval from a judge. This protection is essential to any society that values liberty.

Responsibility and Moral Character

Personal responsibility is a key part of freedom. God created us with the ability to choose right from wrong, so liberty and accountability belong together.[12] People must learn to govern themselves before they can help govern a nation.

Responsible citizens strive to practice honesty, self-control, hard work, and care for others. They support their families, serve in their communities, and accept the results of their choices. When people act responsibly,

---

[12] See 2 Nephi 2:26–27.

government needs less control, and society becomes stronger.

The Constitution reflects this idea by trusting people to guide their own lives. It gives government certain powers but leaves most decisions to individuals, families, and local communities. This system depends on people using their freedom wisely.

Freedom lasts best when citizens act with virtue. Liberty is not the ability to do anything you want. It is choosing what is right and accepting the consequences. The founders taught that freedom requires honesty, courage, and commitment to the common good. Moral character strengthens families, protects communities, and prevents abuse of freedom.

A free nation depends on people who seek to act with integrity. Without virtue, freedom weakens, and society begins to fall apart.

Why This Matters

Freedom depends on strong character. When people act responsibly, families become stronger, communities work better, and government does not need to expand to control what citizens refuse to control themselves. Your choices help protect liberty for yourself and the people around you.

Personal Liberties

Personal liberties are the basic freedoms every person has because each of us has God given worth. These freedoms include speech, religion, the press, the right to assemble, and the right to follow your conscience. These rights allow people to make choices, speak truth, and enjoy the benefits of their efforts. The founders added them to the Bill of Rights to make sure government could never take them away.

A free society depends on these liberties. They allow people to worship, express ideas, and seek truth without fear. These freedoms also strengthen families and communities by encouraging responsibility and respectful cooperation.

Property rights are also an important liberty. When people can own what they earn or create, they gain independence and the ability to provide for their families more effectively. This encourages hard work, saving, and planning for the future. Protecting property rights supports strong families, economic freedom, and the pursuit of happiness.

WHY THIS MATTERS

Personal liberties protect your ability to think, speak, worship, and live according to your beliefs. They give you room to grow, to learn truth, and to become the person God created you to be. When these freedoms are strong, people succeed and communities stay healthy. When they weaken, government gains more control and personal freedom shrinks.

Freedom of Association

Freedom of association allows people to gather, form groups, and work together for shared beliefs and goals in a natural and voluntary way. It protects your right to join clubs, churches, charities, sports teams, and community organizations. This freedom is essential because it helps people build strong relationships and solve problems through cooperation. When people can gather freely, they can also speak more effectively, support one another, and defend their rights.

WHY THIS MATTERS

Freedom of association matters because most good things in society happen when people work together voluntarily. It strengthens families, churches, schools, and neighborhoods. It gives you the ability to stand with others in defense of truth and moral values.

Family, the Foundation of Society

The family is the basic unit of society.[13] It is in families that children first learn honesty, respect, hard work, and responsibility. Strong families help young people grow into responsible citizens who can serve their communities and protect the freedoms they receive. Healthy families build stable communities.

Government should support families, not replace them. Families help teach the values that make self-government possible. They build stable relationships and help each generation learn the importance of duty and care.

A society becomes stronger when it strengthens families, faith, and virtue. When these foundations are weakened,

---

[13] See "The Family: A Proclamation to the World," ChurchofJesusChrist.org.

the whole nation becomes less stable and less prepared to face challenges.

WHY THIS MATTERS

Families shape character long before schools or government policies do. When families are strong, children learn the values that make freedom work. When families weaken, communities struggle, and government grows to fill the gaps. Protecting families protects the future strength of the nation.

Power Begins with the People

In America, government power begins with the people because they consent to it. This was a new idea in a world where rulers often claimed authority through birth, wealth, force, or tradition. The founders rejected that idea and taught that government exists only because citizens give it permission. Power rises from the people upward, not from leaders downward. This means officials serve only with the people's consent and can be replaced when they fail to do what is right.

Because power starts with the people, citizens carry important responsibilities. They must stay informed, participate honestly, and serve in their communities. Leaders are public servants who must follow the Constitution and respect the people who elected them. When citizens understand their own authority, they protect their rights and keep government accountable. A nation stays strong when its people know that their voice matters and when they take part in shaping their future.

Why This Matters

When you understand that power comes from the people, you can see that your voice and your choices matter. You help protect freedom when you learn about the issues, vote wisely, and serve your community. A free nation depends on citizens who take responsibility and hold leaders accountable.

Limited Government

Government should be strong enough to protect rights but limited enough to protect personal freedom, support families and communities, and respect local decisions. Limited government helps people take responsibility for their own lives instead of depending on government for every need. The Constitution gives government only specific powers. When government stays within those limits, freedom grows. When it reaches beyond them, liberty weakens.

Big Government Weakens the People

Government becomes less effective when it begins to do for people what individuals and families can do for themselves. A growing government can weaken responsibility, discourage initiative, and replace the work of families and communities. Excessive government programs and regulations can make people feel dependent rather than empowered. This undermines the basic values that are essential for a free society. The gospel teaches self-reliance, [14] which gives people confidence and strength. Good laws should be simple, moral, and aimed at protecting rights. Too many rules create confusion and make life harder for families and local communities.

A free society needs a government that protects liberty while avoiding unnecessary control over personal choices. When government grows too large, it treats citizens as people to manage instead of individuals with agency. Limited government keeps power close to the people and helps protect dignity and independence.

Once government expands, it rarely gives up its authority willingly. Programs that were originally intended to solve temporary problems often become permanent. Agencies that were created for narrow purposes frequently grow into large departments with broad authority. As the government expands, it often demands more money, which can lead to higher taxes and larger national debt. This places a burden on future generations who must pay for the decisions of the present.

Solve Problems At the Lowest Level

Problems should be solved by the smallest group that can handle them. Local families, churches, and communities usually know the needs of their people best. If a city cannot solve a problem, then a county or state

---

[14] See "Self-Reliance" in Topics and Questions, ChurchofJesusChrist.org and *General Handbook*, 22.1.

may step in. The federal government should act only when no smaller unit can do the job.

When government grows too large, power moves away from the people. Citizens may stop helping with local concerns because they assume national programs will do the work. This weakens civic involvement and reduces the shared responsibility that keeps a free nation strong. Freedom requires participation. People must vote, serve, and care for their neighbors. Government should support families and communities, not replace them.

Government Spending and National Debt

Government should live within its means just as individuals are expected to do. When a nation takes on too much debt, it becomes less independent and more willing to spend irresponsibly. Heavy borrowing hides the true cost of poor decisions and shifts the burden to future generations. Excessive national debt weakens the economy and places avoidable pressure on children who will have to pay for the choices made today.

Why This Matters

Limited government protects your freedom to make choices, raise a family, and live according to your beliefs. When power stays close to the people, communities grow stronger and individuals develop responsibility. When government becomes too large, freedom shrinks and citizens lose the ability to guide their own lives.

Separation of Powers

History shows that concentrated power often leads to corruption and unfair treatment.[15] The founders of America understood this and worked to divide power among branches and levels of government so that no single person or group could control everything.[16]

Separation of powers means that government authority is divided into different branches, each with its own duties and limits. The lawmaking power belongs to Congress, the enforcement power belongs to the President, and the interpretive power belongs to the courts. This structure protects liberty because it prevents the rise of a ruler who can use government power without restraint. It also encourages accountability because each branch must follow the Constitution and cannot claim complete authority. Learn more in chapter 6, "How the Three Branches of Government Work."

Why This Matters

Separation of powers protects your freedom by making sure that no single leader or group can take too much control of the government. It keeps authority spread out so that decisions must be debated and reviewed. This structure helps preserve stability, fairness, and trust in the system. When power is divided, liberty is safer.

---

[15] Doctrine and Covenants 121:39

[16] The Federalist Papers No. 10 and No. 51 emphasize the dangers of unchecked power and the need for balanced institutions.

Checks and Balances

Checks and balances give each branch of government the ability to limit the others. Congress creates laws, but the President may veto them. The courts can decide whether laws follow the Constitution. The Senate must approve certain appointments made by the President. These interactions help prevent any branch from acting alone or ignoring its limits. The founders designed this structure so that one person's ambition would limit another's ambition, and so that every part of government would have reasons to cooperate.

Why This Matters

Checks and balances helps keep government honest. They protect you by making sure no single branch becomes too powerful or makes decisions without proper oversight. This provides a system where government must act carefully and within constitutional boundaries.

Judicial Review

Judicial review is the power of the courts to decide whether laws or government actions follow the Constitution. If a law violates a person's rights or gives government too much power, the courts can declare the law invalid. Judges do not create laws, but they ensure that laws and government leaders stay within the limits of the Constitution.

Why This Matters

Judicial review safeguards your rights by making sure that even well-meaning laws do not contradict the Constitution. It also holds leaders accountable and prevents government from acting outside its authority. This protection helps maintain a free and stable society.

Federalism

Federalism means that power is shared between the national government and the states. This system protects freedom by preventing any one level of government from gaining too much control. The founders chose federalism because they knew that concentrated power often leads to abuse. The Constitution limits the national government to specific responsibilities and leaves all remaining powers to the states or to the people.[17]

Federalism also supports the idea that communities should solve problems close to home whenever they can. It allows states to keep their own identity while still working together as one nation.

Why This Matters

Federalism keeps government power balanced and close to the people. It allows states to meet local needs while the nation remains united in protecting rights and liberty. When power is shared wisely, freedom is safer and communities can thrive.

States' Rights and Local Self-Government

States have their own rights and responsibilities. Early Americans were used to governing themselves in towns, churches, and state assemblies, and they had done this

---

[17] United States Constitution, amendment 10.

for generations. The founders wanted to protect this tradition because it taught responsibility, cooperation, and civic virtue. Local governments and community institutions help shape character and prepare people to take part in national life.

Why This Matters

States' rights help keep government power close to the people. When local communities make many of their own decisions, citizens stay more involved and have a stronger voice, and freedom is easier to protect. Sharing authority strengthens both the nation and the communities within it.

Federal Supremacy (Within Its Limits)

Federal supremacy means that the Constitution is the highest law of the land and that state laws must follow it. This principle keeps the nation united under a shared framework. It ensures that every citizen enjoys the same constitutional protections, no matter where they live. Federal supremacy does not erase local authority. Instead, it creates a clear foundation that all government levels must follow, while still allowing states to solve local problems.

Why This Matters

Federal supremacy protects your rights from being weakened by state laws that might conflict with the Constitution. It keeps the country stable and prevents conflicts between states. It also ensures fairness by making sure that all people are protected equally under the same Constitution.

Capitalism and Free Markets

Capitalism and free markets encourage people to work hard, be creative, and solve problems. When individuals and families can make their own economic choices, prosperity grows. Too much government control slows progress and weakens innovation.

Government should support private enterprise instead of replacing it. Families, businesses, and local communities often handle economic needs better than large national programs. Leaders like Alexander Hamilton helped build a financial system that rewards responsibility and supports economic growth.

Free markets allow competition and choice, which raise living standards and strengthen communities. They also support generosity. When people are free to prosper, they are better able to help their families, give to charity, and serve others.

Why This Matters

Free markets give people the chance to improve their lives through effort and responsibility. They encourage creativity and independence while giving people and communities the resources they need to serve one another. A strong economy strengthens freedom because it allows people to build secure lives, help others, and pursue opportunities without depending on government for every need.

Equal Rights, Not Equal Results

Government should protect equal rights, not guarantee equal results. Fairness means equal treatment under the law, not identical outcomes. People have different talents, interests, and circumstances, so it is natural that their results will differ. When government tries to force everyone to end up the same, it must control choices and limit personal freedoms.

Protecting equal rights gives every person the chance to work, grow, and succeed according to their abilities. It prevents discrimination while still rewarding effort and responsibility. In a free society, government should protect liberty and justice. It should make sure everyone has the same legal protections and opportunities, not manage people's lives to produce matching outcomes.

Why This Matters

Equal rights protect freedom because they give everyone a fair start without forcing everyone to finish the same way. This encourages personal responsibility, rewards hard work, and allows people to pursue their goals in their own way. When government focuses on equal results instead of equal rights, freedom shrinks and personal choices become limited.

Religious Freedom

Freedom of religion is a basic human right and the first right protected by the Constitution. It allows people to think, speak, and live according to their beliefs without fear.[18] It protects believers and nonbelievers and helps a diverse society stay peaceful and strong.

Religion plays an important role in strengthening individuals and communities. For faith to do good, people need room in daily life and in the law to practice their beliefs. Every lawful voice should be welcome in public life. Religion is more than private worship. It includes sharing beliefs, teaching values, and speaking about moral issues.

Religious freedom does not mean forcing religious ideas into government. It means government should not interfere with a person's sincere practice of faith.

What You Can Do

Religious freedom is weakening in many parts of the world. Churches, groups, and individuals sometimes face pressure or limits on expressing their beliefs. Still, caring people can help protect this freedom.

Religious freedom is both a right and a responsibility. It requires respect for others and for their dignity. People should share their beliefs kindly and in a respectful way.

- Learn what religious freedom is and why it is important.
- Practice it by respecting others' beliefs and being civil in conversations.

---

[18] See "Religious Freedom," in Newsroom.ChurchofJesusChrist.org and "Religious Freedom" in Topics and Questions, ChurchofJesusChrist.org.

- Support it by participating in your community and teaching others why it matters.

WHY THIS MATTERS

Religious freedom allows you to worship God, live your beliefs, and speak truth without fear. It protects people, strengthens moral values, and encourages kindness in a diverse society. When this freedom is strong, people of all faiths can live together with respect. When it weakens, personal agency and moral voice are placed at risk.

CHAPTER 6

How the Three Branches of Government Work

The Constitution of the United States created a system of government designed to protect liberty, prevent abuse of power, and encourage cooperation. The founders believed that power should not rest in one place. They divided authority so that each branch could limit the others and protect the principles of the American founding.

The founders understood human nature. They recognized that people can do great good but can also act selfishly at times. Because of this, they created a structure that separates powers and uses checks and balances, so that no branch becomes too strong. Each branch has its own responsibilities and limits, and each one can restrain the others when needed.

The three branches of government are the legislative branch, the executive branch, and the judicial branch. Each branch faces different political pressures. The president is chosen by electors, Senators were originally chosen by state legislatures, representatives are elected by the people, and Supreme Court justices are appointed by the president with the consent of the Senate. This system was carefully designed to make it difficult for any single group or majority of the people to control the government.

The Legislative Branch: Congress

The legislative branch makes the laws that govern the nation. It has two parts, the House of Representatives and the Senate.

- *The House of Representatives* represents the people directly. Each state has a number of representatives based on the population of the state. Members serve two-year terms, which helps them stay close to the needs and concerns of the people.
- *The Senate* represents the states. Each state has two senators, no matter its population. Senators serve six-year terms, which gives stability and encourages long-term thinking.

This two-part Congress was created through careful compromise. It protected the equal voice of the states while still respecting population differences. The founders designed this balanced system to encourage fairness and protect freedom.

How Congress Creates Laws

1. A bill is introduced in either the House or the Senate.
2. Committees study the bill, debate it, and may make changes.
3. The full House or Senate votes on it.
4. If both houses pass the same version, the bill is sent to the President.

5. If the President signs it, it becomes law. If the President vetoes it, Congress can override the veto with a two-thirds vote in both houses.

This process encourages patience, cooperation, and careful decision making among elected representatives. It also helps prevent sudden or impulsive laws.

The Executive Branch: The President

The executive branch carries out the laws that Congress passes. This branch includes the President, the Vice President, and many departments and agencies.

Responsibilities of the President

The President has several key responsibilities:

- Enforcing federal laws
- Serving as Commander in Chief of the military.
- Managing relationships with other nations.
- Appointing judges, ambassadors, and cabinet leaders.
- Signing or vetoing bills from Congress.

At the Constitutional Convention, the delegates debated the executive branch carefully. They feared unchecked power but knew the nation needed strong and unified leadership. They trusted George Washington to set an example of humility and restraint. His leadership helped define what it means to be a constitutional President.

Limits on the Executive Branch

The President's power is limited in several ways:

- The Senate must approve treaties and many appointments.
- Congress controls government funding.
- Congress can impeach and remove a President for serious wrongdoing.
- The courts can declare executive actions unconstitutional.

These limits help ensure that the President serves the people rather than the people serving the President.

The Judicial Branch: The Supreme Court and Federal Courts

The judicial branch interprets the laws. It ensures that laws and government actions follow the Constitution.

- *The Supreme Court* is the highest court in the nation. It hears cases involving constitutional questions, disputes between states, and other major issues. Its decisions set precedents that guide all other courts and help keep the laws consistent across the country.
- *Federal courts* hear cases that involve federal law, disputes between citizens from different states, and questions about the Constitution. They help ensure that national laws are applied fairly and consistently.

Leaders such as John Jay and John Marshall strengthened the role of the courts. Their work helped establish the judicial branch so that everyone would be expected to obey the laws. They understood that freedom depends on stable and fair courts that apply laws equally to everyone.

LIMITS ON THE JUDICIAL BRANCH

- Judges are appointed by the President and must be confirmed by the Senate.
- Congress can change the structure of lower federal courts.
- Courts depend on the executive branch to carry out their decisions.

These limits keep the judicial branch balanced and accountable within the constitutional system.

Why Three Branches Matter

Dividing power helps protect freedom. When each branch has its own duties and limits, government becomes more fair, stable, and accountable. Citizens benefit because decisions are not controlled by one person or group. Shared power encourages cooperation and helps protect our rights.

This system is one of the great achievements of the American founding. It reflects a thoughtful understanding of human nature and a sincere desire to preserve liberty for future generations.

CHAPTER 7

Political Parties

Political parties play an important role in American government. They bring together people who share similar ideas about how the country should be run. While several parties exist, the Democratic Party and the Republican Party are the two major parties. Smaller parties also take part in elections and may influence certain issues. Parties help voters understand where candidates stand and how they might lead the nation.

Parties hold debates, propose solutions, and represent different viewpoints. They help organize political life, although they do not replace your responsibility to think for yourself. It can be helpful to prayerfully decide which issues matter most and look for candidates who serve with integrity. Principles matter more than party labels, and character matters more than political identity in the long run. When citizens remember this, freedom is easier to protect.

Every political party has a written platform. A platform explains what the party believes, what policies it supports, and what goals it hopes to achieve. Platforms cover issues such as taxes, healthcare, education, national security, the environment, and social concerns. They are updated regularly and help voters compare ideas and promises.

Because there are many political issues, you may not agree with a party on every topic. You may agree with some positions and disagree with others. Your views may align with one party in one election and another party in a future election. This is why it is helpful to study platforms for yourself and compare them with your values and beliefs.

Political parties can also provide ways to participate in government. You can write to leaders, volunteer in campaigns, attend local meetings, ask questions, and share your views respectfully. These actions can help shape your community and your country. You can support honest and wise candidates who reflect your values, even if they belong to different parties.

Democratic Party

The Democratic Party generally supports a larger role for the federal government. It favors expanding welfare, healthcare, and social programs for all Americans. These initiatives would be funded in part by requiring the wealthiest Americans and large corporations to pay higher taxes, while advancing racial and economic equity. It strongly supports protecting and expanding abortion rights and making historic investments to combat the climate crisis.

Learn about the Democratic platform at democrats.org and ballotpedia.org.

Republican Party

The Republican Party supports limited government, tax relief for working Americans, strong national defense, and safeguarding constitutional rights and traditional values. Its platform focuses on securing the border and stopping illegal immigration, reducing inflation, restoring affordability, achieving energy independence, bringing back manufacturing, cutting taxes and regulations, strengthening public safety, modernizing the military, protecting Social Security and Medicare, and ensuring that elections are secure.

Learn about the Republican platform at 2024gopplatform.com and ballotpedia.org.

Why This Matters

Understanding how political parties work can help you make sense of the news and the choices you face as a voter. By learning about party platforms and studying issues for yourself, you can form your own beliefs instead of following someone else's opinions.

Voting is important because your choices help shape the society you are part of. Learning about parties, platforms, and issues prepares you to vote wisely. It also can give you confidence to speak respectfully about civic matters, support good candidates, and stand for truth.

CHAPTER 8

Different Systems of Government

The kind of government a nation chooses shapes the quality of life its people experience. America's founders knew from history that some systems protect freedom while others can threaten it. They studied earlier civilizations, European monarchies, and philosophical writings to learn what strengthens a nation and what leads to oppression. They believed the United States should follow principles that honor human dignity, protect natural rights, and encourage responsibility.

This chapter compares four key systems of government to help you understand why the founders created a constitutional republic. It also explains why they warned against systems like socialism, Marxism, and communism. Many countries today mix different systems of government, combining parts of socialism with democratic institutions.

Constitutional Republic

A constitutional republic is the system established by the United States Constitution. In a republic, the people elect representatives who make decisions based on a written constitution. The Constitution limits government power and protects individual rights.

Key features of a constitutional republic include:

- Leaders are elected by the people.
- Government power is limited by a written constitution.
- Rights come from God, not the government.
- Power is divided to prevent any group from taking control.
- Leaders and citizens are expected to obey the same laws.

A *constitutional republic* is different from a *pure democracy* primarily in how power is limited and protected.

- In a *pure democracy,* people vote directly on every issue, and the majority can make decisions even if they harm minority rights. This can lead to "mob rule," where majority groups can oppress minorities, confiscate property, or exert their views without restraint. Historical examples of pure democracies, such as ancient Athens, show that they often become unstable because groups compete for power and there are not enough protections to keep the peace.
- In a *constitutional republic,* like the United States, the people are the source of authority, but they choose representatives to make laws. The Constitution protects individual rights that cannot be removed by a majority vote. Separation of powers, checks and balances, judicial review, federalism, and the Bill of

Rights all help prevent abuses of power. This system ensures that everyone obeys the same laws.

The founders, including James Madison[19], designed this system to avoid the dangers of pure democracy and to protect personal freedom. A constitutional republic keeps majority rule in balance with strong protection for individual rights.

Why the Founders Chose This System

The founders taught that a republic is one of the best ways to protect both liberty and order. In a republic, citizens take part in public life while avoiding the dangers that come when too much power gathers in one place. A republic also depends on virtue, moral responsibility, and strong families. These qualities help keep freedom steady and secure through the years. A constitutional republic reflects the values of self-government, personal agency, and accountability.

Socialism

Socialism is a system where the government owns or controls major parts of the economy, including industries, businesses, and resources. Its goal is to create greater equality by allowing the government to direct economic life.

Key features of socialism include:

---

[19] See Federalist No. 10. Madison warned that pure democracies would create contention and not safeguard personal security or the rights of property.

- Strong government control over the economy.
- Economic decisions made by central planners instead of individuals and families.
- Limited private ownership.
- Redistribution of wealth through government programs.
- Restricted personal freedoms and political rights.

Different countries apply socialist ideas in different ways and produce different outcomes.

Concerns with Socialism

Economic problems. Some people present socialism as a way to make life more affordable, yet in practice many countries with strong government control of the economy have faced declines in living standards. Countries that place strict government control over major economic decisions have frequently faced shortages, inefficiency, and long periods of stagnation. In China, Chairman Mao's socialist economic policies led to crisis and widespread famine, which eventually pushed the government to shift toward market-based reforms. After World War Two, Britain nationalized many major industries, and the economy struggled for decades until significant market reforms began in the 1980s. Cuba continues to experience long-term shortages of food and fuel, and the country depends heavily on support from Russia to meet basic needs. Venezuela was once one of the wealthiest nations in Latin America, yet years of extensive state control contributed to a severe economic collapse.

Equality. Although socialism teaches equality, many socialist governments have created new inequalities because political leaders often enjoy better access to goods and services than ordinary citizens. Policies that rely on forced redistribution of wealth can weaken trust and reduce self-reliance, since people may feel less motivated to work hard when rewards do not match effort.

Freedoms and rights. In practice, many socialist governments have restricted personal freedoms and political rights. Stalin's Soviet Union used secret police, labor camps, and executions to control the population during his rule. The Soviet Union finally collapsed in 1991 after many years of political and economic problems. In Eastern Europe, socialist governments limited political rights until the fall of the Berlin Wall in 1989 and the end of Soviet control. After the Castro brothers took power in Cuba in 1959, political freedoms were greatly reduced, and over time nearly one third of all Cubans left the island in search of better conditions

Why This Matters

When the government makes most economic decisions, people often lose the freedom to choose for themselves. Economic freedom supports dignity, creativity, and opportunity. In many countries with strict government control, citizens become more dependent on government programs and may lose the incentive to work and innovate. Some socialist governments have also claimed that socialism is the first step toward full communism. Stalin's Soviet Union, for example, called itself a socialist state, but the government controlled nearly every part of life, and leaders taught that socialism had to be created before communism could ever be achieved.

Marxism

Marxism is a political and economic theory developed by Karl Marx. It teaches that society is divided into classes and that history is shaped by conflict between the rich and the poor. Marxism claims that removing private property would end this struggle.

Key features of Marxism include:

- Viewing society as a struggle between groups.
- Rejecting private property.
- Supporting revolution to replace existing institutions.
- Calling for government control of major economic and social systems.

Concerns with Marxism

The American founders rejected the idea that society is defined by class conflict. They believed that people are equal in dignity and should have the ability to rise through hard work, not through government force. In practice, Marxism has often removed basic freedoms, weakened families, and replaced individual agency with state control.

Communism

Communism is Marxism put fully into practice. In a communist system, the government owns all property, controls all production, and directs nearly every part of the economy. There is no private ownership, no free markets, and very little personal freedom.

Key features of communism include:

- Complete government ownership of property and resources.
- No private property rights.
- Strong limits on religion, speech, and movement.
- Central planning instead of individual choices.
- Very limited power for citizens to influence government.

Consequences of Communism

Many communist governments throughout history have resulted in hardship, loss of freedom, and various forms of oppression. Because the government controls everything, people cannot freely choose their work, worship, or family life. Countries such as the Soviet Union, Maoist China, North Korea, Cuba, and nations in Eastern Europe are examples of communism where the people experienced shortages, repression, and widespread limits on liberty.

Unlimited government power can become a serious threat to human freedom. Government should serve the people, not rule every part of their lives. Communism stands in direct opposition to these principles.

Why These Comparisons Matter

Understanding different systems of government helps you appreciate the wisdom of America's founders. They chose a constitutional republic because it protects natural rights, encourages virtue, limits government power, and supports strong families and individuals.

A constitutional republic supports important principles such as personal agency, responsibility, moral freedom, obeying the law, opportunity through hard work, and strong local communities.

Systems like socialism, Marxism, and communism often work against these principles. They tend to replace personal responsibility with government control. They can weaken families, suppress freedom, and reduce human dignity by treating people as subjects of the state instead of as children of God.

When you understand these differences, you can better value the blessings of freedom and the responsibilities that come with living in a free society.

CHAPTER 9

Methods of Government Control

The previous chapter described systems of government—constitutional republics, socialism, Marxism, and communism. This chapter explains that regardless of the ideological system of government, there are various ways that governments may exercise power.

Understanding these methods of control is often as important as knowing the ideologies behind them. A nation may claim to be a republic, a socialist state, or a democracy and still restrict freedom or concentrate power.

The way a government uses power often reveals much about its true character. Many governments in history have drifted toward authoritarian or totalitarian practices. Learning to recognize these patterns helps people identify threats to liberty before they grow too strong.

Authoritarianism

Authoritarianism is a system where power is held by one ruler or a small group. Elections, if they exist at all, are tightly controlled, and citizens often have very limited influence on government decisions. Basic freedoms such as speech, assembly, and the press may exist on paper but are restricted in practice.

Key characteristics of authoritarianism include:

- Power centered in one leader or ruling group.
- Controlled or limited elections.
- Suppression of political opposition.
- Restrictions on individual freedoms.

Examples include Francoist Spain, military juntas in Argentina and Chile, and the rule of Nicolás Maduro in Venezuela, where opposition was repressed and media was tightly controlled.

Authoritarian governments often claim they are protecting order or unity, although history suggests that leaders who gain concentrated power rarely give it up willingly.

Totalitarianism

Totalitarianism is one of the most extreme forms of government control. In a totalitarian system, the government tries to control nearly every part of life, including politics, education, religion, family choices, and even personal beliefs. It often uses propaganda, surveillance, and fear to shape how people act and think.

Key characteristics of totalitarianism include:

- Control of speech, media, and information.
- Government control of education, culture, and religion.

- Pressure on people to show loyalty to the state above all else.
- Use of surveillance and intimidation to force obedience.

Examples include Stalin's Soviet Union, Nazi Germany, and modern North Korea.

Although communism has often led to totalitarian systems, totalitarianism can also appear under many ideologies, including extreme nationalism, theocracy, or militarism.

Monarchy

A monarchy is a system where one person holds power, usually passed down through a family line. Some monarchies today, like in Great Britain, are mostly ceremonial and work within a constitutional system. Others are absolute monarchies, where the ruler has full political authority. The American founders lived under the abuses of monarchical power under King George III and chose a constitutional republic instead.

Key characteristics of monarchy include:

- Power held by a single ruler, often for life.
- Political authority inherited rather than earned.
- Rights depending on the will of the monarch.
- Limited influence for citizens on government decisions.

Examples include pre-Revolutionary France and imperial Russia, where rulers controlled lawmaking, taxation, religion, and national policy. The American founders rejected monarchy because they believed political power should come from the people rather than from birth or privilege.

Oligarchy

An oligarchy is a system in which a small group holds political or economic power. This group may include wealthy families, military leaders, political elites, or party officials. Oligarchies may claim to represent the people, but they limit participation to their own circle.

Key characteristics of oligarchy include:

- Power held by a small ruling group.
- Decisions are often made in ways that benefit elites.
- Limited competition or open dissent.
- Few opportunities for ordinary citizens to gain influence.

Examples include the former Soviet Union, which was controlled by a small Communist Party elite, and modern authoritarian states where wealthy or powerful groups strongly influence government decisions.

Oligarchy can form within many types of systems. Socialist, Marxist, and communist governments can become oligarchies when power concentrates in the hands of party leaders.

Why These Methods of Control Matter

Understanding these methods of control helps people notice early warning signs when a government may be moving toward too much control. A nation may claim to be free or democratic yet still restrict speech, monitor citizens, centralize power, or pressure people to conform. By learning how authoritarianism, totalitarianism, monarchy, and oligarchy work, you can better understand why the founders created so many safeguards in the American system. Protecting liberty requires steady awareness and responsible citizens.

CHAPTER 10

Political Ideologies

Political ideologies influence how governments act and how people understand human nature, personal responsibility, the role of government, and the proper balance between personal responsibility and societal control. Some ideologies support freedom, virtue, and strong communities. Others create dependence on government, pressure people to conform, or weaken families and local institutions.

Why Understanding These Ideologies Matters

Ideologies shape culture before they shape government. They influence how people view truth, responsibility, family, and freedom. Some ideas strengthen liberty by encouraging virtue, self-reliance, and respect for natural law. Others weaken liberty by expanding government control, redefining moral standards, or placing personal desires above the common good.

By learning about these ideologies, you can recognize which ideas protect freedom and which ones threaten it. Staying informed and grounded in true principles helps preserve liberty for future generations.

Gender Ideology

Gender ideology is a modern way of thinking that teaches that gender is not fixed or purely biological and is not rooted in natural law. Instead, it says that gender is a personal identity that may change based on a person's feelings or sense of self. This idea influences how governments approach education, parental rights, healthcare, sports, and public facilities. Policies based on gender ideology often attempt to redefine the legal meaning of male and female, which affects how laws are written and applied.

Transgender ideology is a part of gender ideology and promotes the idea that people can transition between sexes. It proposes that a person's gender identity can override their biological sex. It supports social and medical steps to help people live according to their chosen identity.

Government Policies

People are free to believe as they choose, but problems arise when government policies require schools, families, or citizens to adopt those beliefs by law or regulation.

When governments adopt transgender ideology, they may create policies that come into conflict with parental rights, children's privacy and safety, the fairness of women's sports, and access to dressing rooms and public restrooms. Schools may be pressured to teach gender ideas that many families do not support. Medical treatments may be offered to minors without parental consent or without long-term evidence of safety. Rules about preferred speech or pronouns can also create pressure for individuals to accept beliefs they do not personally share.

Every person deserves respect and compassion, but government policies based on transgender ideology can lead to laws and cultural pressures that reduce freedom of conscience, deny basic biological truths, and weaken the role of families in guiding their children.

Gospel Teachings

The restored gospel teaches that gender is an essential part of Heavenly Father's plan of happiness.[20] Some people feel their inner sense of gender does not match their biological sex at birth. Some people who experience these feelings may identify as transgender. These individuals often face real and very difficult challenges. They and their families should always be treated with kindness, compassion, and Christlike love. All people are children of God and have divine worth.

Why This Matters

Understanding gender ideology matters because it affects many parts of everyday life. These ideas influence what schools teach, how sports are organized, how bathrooms and locker rooms are assigned, and even what words you may be asked to use. You will meet people with different beliefs about gender. Knowing what you personally believe, what the scriptures teach, and how to show kindness can help you stay grounded in truth while still treating others with love.

---

[20] See Genesis 1:27 and "The Family: A Proclamation to the World." For Church policies regarding people who identify as transgender, see *General Handbook,* 38.6.23.

Gender ideology also affects your freedom to think, speak, and act according to your conscience. When governments or institutions adopt these ideas, they may create rules that make you feel pressured to accept things you do not believe. Learning to understand different viewpoints while keeping your own values can help you become a strong, confident, and compassionate disciple of Jesus Christ. It prepares you to live in a world with many voices while staying true to the purpose and identity God has given you.

Progressivism

Progressivism developed long after the American founding and has changed over time. Progressivism in the early twentieth century focused on cleaner elections, reducing corruption, and improving public health. Modern progressivism is different. It often supports expanding the power of the national government and relying on experts and large agencies to direct policy rather than leaving most decisions to citizens and elected representatives.

Many people who support progressive policies do so because they sincerely want to help others, yet their proposed solutions often rely on expanded government power that can lead to weakened liberty. The founders of America built the republic on natural rights, limited government, and personal responsibility. They knew that people are capable of both good and evil, so they believed that government should be limited because those in power often seek more authority than is wise.

Progressivism and the Constitution

One concern with modern progressivism is its view of the Constitution. Progressives often teach that the Constitution should be a living and flexible document that changes with the times. This may sound reasonable to some, but the founders designed the Constitution to protect permanent principles rather than shifting public opinions. They believed the Constitution should restrain government and protect individual rights.

The founders also taught that changes should come through formal amendments, not through reinterpretation by judges or government officials. When the Constitution is treated as something that can be reinterpreted by judges or government officials, the limits that protect liberty can become weaker.

Growing Government Control

Progressive policies often encourage the growth of large administrative agencies. The founders were cautious about concentrated power and tried to prevent it through federalism and the separation of powers. Modern progressivism often shifts authority away from elected representatives and gives it to government agencies led by unelected officials.

These agencies create rules that can affect many areas of life, including education, environmental regulations, building permits, and business licensing. When unelected officials make these rules, the role of citizens can become weaker, and the power of the government can grow.

Individual Responsibility

Progressive policies often shift responsibility from individuals to government programs. Some government help is necessary and compassionate but extensive programs can become permanent and create dependency. This dependency reduces personal initiative and shifts expectations away from hard work and community support. Free people must take responsibility for their choices and develop self-reliance.

Church leaders teach that individuals and families have the primary duty to care for their own needs. When people practice principles of self-reliance, they are better prepared to solve future needs on their own. When people cannot care for themselves, they are encouraged to first seek help from extended family, then from church or government programs.[21]

When government takes over too many responsibilities, it removes opportunities for individuals and families to serve one another. People also lose the blessings that come from charitable giving when government agencies decide how resources are distributed. Service, family support, and voluntary charity can strengthen communities more effectively than government programs.

Role of Religion

America's founders believed that religion and morality are essential to preserving freedom. Modern progressive

---

[21] See *General Handbook,* 22.4.1.

policies can weaken the role of religion and traditional moral teaching in public life. Many progressives argue that government should be morally neutral and that public institutions should avoid promoting traditional moral values. However, religion and virtue provide important moral foundations for society. They guide citizens, encourage responsibility, and help restrain harmful behavior. When moral and religious voices are pushed aside, society loses guidance that helps protect freedom and stability.

Economic Issues

Progressivism often seeks economic equality through regulation, but heavy regulation can limit economic freedom and slow innovation. Progressive policies tend to increase government rules, which can raise costs, slow innovation, and reduce competition over time. This often leads to higher taxes and government-directed solutions that limit the freedom of businesses and individuals to innovate and solve problems.

Free markets work differently. They encourage creativity, reward effort, and allow people to improve their lives. Leaders such as Alexander Hamilton believed that economic freedom strengthens the nation. Modern progressive policies often move in the opposite direction by giving more control to government planners instead of families, workers, and entrepreneurs.

Natural Law

Progressivism often weakens the belief that truth is eternal and that rights come from God rather than from government. It teaches that rights and laws should change with culture, public opinion, or political movements. This approach can create inconsistent standards and weaken the stability of important institutions.

Summary

Progressivism seeks to solve social problems, but some of its approaches can unintentionally conflict with the principles that protect liberty and personal responsibility. It can expand government power, weaken constitutional limits, and may undermine personal responsibility and reduce the role of moral values. It can also shift authority away from families, communities, and individual citizens. A free nation must protect the structures and values that keep government within proper limits. Progressivism challenges these safeguards and can make it harder to preserve liberty for future generations.

Why This Matters

Understanding progressivism matters because it influences many parts of everyday life. It shapes what schools teach, how regulations are made, and how much control government has over families and communities. Some progressive ideas encourage government officials and experts to make decisions that used to belong to parents, local communities, or individuals. When this happens, people may lose some of the freedom to make personal choices or live according to their beliefs.

Learning about progressivism also helps you see the difference between solving problems through personal responsibility and solving them through government control. It shows why the founders limited government power and why the gospel teaches self-reliance, family involvement, and strong moral character. When you understand these ideas, you can make wise choices, recognize when freedom may be at risk, and stay grounded in the values that lead to lasting happiness and liberty.

Extreme Environmentalism

Environmental stewardship is important. We should care for the earth, use its resources wisely, and preserve it for future generations. Most people see this as a basic moral responsibility.

Extreme environmentalism goes beyond responsible care when it places nature above people and overlooks the scriptural truth that human beings are central to God's creation.

Climate Change

Public discussions about climate change often include dramatic predictions of catastrophic events. Over the past 50 years, prominent voices in media and advocacy groups have warned about new ice ages, ice free poles, submerged nations, and large-scale famines. Many of these specific predictions have not come to pass. For example, headlines in the 1970s warned of a coming ice age, later predictions suggested that all the ice would be melted from the Arctic by 2013, and some claimed entire island nations would be underwater by the year 2000. These examples show that long-range forecasts can be uncertain and that some claims have been overstated.

You may have heard only the most extreme versions of climate messages. Schools, news outlets, and social media influencers frequently emphasize catastrophic scenarios. When the conversation is driven by fear, it can create anxiety and discourage thoughtful discussion and action. Climate change is an issue that deserves careful study, yet it is important to distinguish reasonable research from alarmist claims.

Population Control

Some environmental activists argue that human population is a major problem and call for population control, limits on family size, or reductions in human activity. These ideas conflict with God's commandment for His children to multiply and replenish the earth. [22]

Extreme Environmental Policies

Because it sees government as the main defender of the planet, extreme environmentalism advocates large regulatory systems that reduce local control and give major decision-making power to government agencies.

When government policies put environmental goals above human needs, they may limit economic freedom, private property rights, and personal lifestyle choices. Government regulations may limit heating sources, restrict what vehicles you can buy, or require costly

---

[22] "The Family: A Proclamation to the World states, "We declare that God's commandment for His children to multiply and replenish the earth remains in force." See ChurchofJesusChrist.org.

upgrades to homes and businesses. These demands can create significant financial burdens for ordinary citizens.

Gospel Teachings

Scripture teaches that God created the earth with abundant resources for His children.[23] He prepared a world filled with plants, animals, water, minerals, and beauty to sustain life and bring joy. God expects us to use these resources wisely, respectfully, and with gratitude. Belief in divine creation builds confidence that the earth has enough to meet our needs when we manage it wisely, rather than fearing that people themselves are the enemy of the planet.

Why This Matters

Extreme environmental ideas matter because they affect daily life. These ideas influence rules about energy, transportation, food production, and even what students learn in school. Some policies help protect the earth, while others can place heavy restrictions, raise costs, and reduce personal choices. Understanding the difference helps you see when environmental policies support freedom and when they begin to take it away.

Extreme environmental policies can increase government power and reduce personal freedom in meaningful ways. Government policies should always be balanced with personal liberty, property rights, and self-reliance. When you understand stewardship and freedom together, you can help protect the earth while also defending the rights

---

[23] Genesis 1:28–31 and Doctrine and Covenants 104:17, 59:16–20.

and opportunities that help individuals and communities to thrive.

Secular Humanism and Relativism

Secular humanism teaches that moral truth comes from human reason alone and that spiritual beliefs should have little or no role in guiding public life. It tends to remove God, faith, and religious morality from schools, laws, and many public institutions. In this view, people become the primary source of truth, and society decides right and wrong based on changing opinions rather than eternal principles.

A major part of secular humanism is relativism, which comes in two forms.

- *Moral relativism* teaches that there is no permanent right or wrong, only personal preferences. It claims that each person can create their own version of truth. This belief leads people to say things like, "My truth is my truth, and your truth is your truth." When this belief spreads, traditional values such as honesty, chastity, service, and self-control may lose importance because they are treated as personal preferences rather than eternal laws.
- *Cultural relativism* teaches that all cultures and moral systems should be viewed as equal, even when they contradict one another. In this view, no culture has the right to claim that any behavior is wrong. It can remove a shared foundation for law or moral

standards and make it difficult for people to agree on principles that protect individuals and freedom.

When moral and cultural relativism replace absolute truth, people may begin to expect government to decide what is acceptable. Government grows larger as it creates rules to replace the moral guidance once taught in homes, churches, and communities. As people rely more on government for moral decisions, personal freedom can become weaker.

Societies that remove God from public life can become confused about right and wrong. Secular humanism discourages expressions of faith, treats spiritual beliefs as outdated, and pressures believers to stay silent. As these ideas spread, religious values may be pushed aside in schools, civic life, and public conversations. People may feel they cannot openly share what they believe without being judged or criticized by others.

The gospel teaches that real wisdom begins with faith in God rather than relying solely on human opinion. Eternal truths do not change with time, culture, or personal preference. God's commandments show His love and lead to happiness. Liberty depends on virtue, and virtue depends on accountability to God. When secular humanism and relativism separate morality from God, one of the strongest foundations of freedom can become weakened.

Why This Matters

Secular humanism and relativism influence much of what you see in school, entertainment, and social media.

These ideas can make it seem as if every opinion has the same value and that spiritual truths should be kept mostly private. When this happens, it becomes harder to know which voices to trust and easier to believe that right and wrong are simply personal choices rather than eternal truths.

Understanding secular humanism and relativism helps you see why some people step away from religious teachings and why society may sometimes treat faith as unimportant. America's founders taught that liberty depends on people who strive to live moral lives. The gospel teaches that truth comes from God and that His commandments lead to happiness. When you understand these principles, you can stay anchored in eternal truth even when the world becomes confused about moral standards. You can also defend your freedom to live your faith openly and respectfully while recognizing the risks that come when truth is left to shifting human opinions.

Radical Individualism

Radical individualism teaches that personal freedom matters more than responsibility, duty, or community. It claims that self-expression and personal fulfillment are the highest goals in life, even when those choices may harm other people or society.

This idea is very different from healthy individual liberty. Liberty is freedom that is organized and protected by law so that everyone's rights can coexist. We can only enjoy true liberty when we exercise self-control and remain accountable for our actions. Personal agency is a gift from God, but it must be used in a way that does not take away from the rights of others.

In a free society, people make choices and accept the consequences. Families, churches, and communities teach about service, sacrifice, patience, and respect. Radical individualism tends to reject these lessons. It often treats obligations to others as burdens instead of blessings. It encourages people to focus on themselves, avoid commitments, and see responsibility as optional. This can make it harder to build strong marriages, raise children in stable homes, and create communities based on trust.

When radical individualism shapes laws and social expectations, institutions like marriage, family, and neighborhoods are weakened. People may treat commitments as temporary rather than as sacred promises. Homes and communities become less stable, and children suffer when adults focus more on personal fulfillment than on providing love and guidance. Communities may lose some of the shared purpose that encourages people to help one another and work for the common good. Strong families build strong societies, but radical individualism can weaken those foundations by placing personal autonomy above relationships and responsibility.

Effect on Government

When families and communities weaken, people often turn to government to solve problems that were once handled by parents, neighbors, churches, and local groups. As people support each other less, government tends to grow to fill the gap. This growth in government power weakens the very freedom that radical individualism claims to protect. Instead of strengthening liberty, it creates conditions where government expands and becomes more involved in daily life.

The founders taught that self-government depends on people who strive to govern themselves. A society that embraces radical individualism may eventually lose both personal and political freedom because people rely more on government and less on their own responsibility.

Gospel Teachings

Radical individualism often conflicts with gospel teachings about discipleship and covenant relationships. Scripture teaches that real happiness comes from loving God and loving others. The Savior taught that we find our lives by serving others, not by seeking only our own desires. The restored gospel also teaches that families are eternal and that parents have sacred duties to their children.

Radical individualism rejects these truths by teaching that personal choice is more important than duty, sacrifice, or God's commandments. This can make it harder for people to grow in Christlike attributes and harder for families to stay strong across generations.

Balanced Individualism

A balanced society benefits from people who understand their own worth, use their agency wisely, and act with confidence. It also needs citizens who know that freedom grows stronger when paired with responsibility. Families depend on commitment, and communities depend on service and cooperation.

When people use liberty selfishly, society can become weaker. When liberty is guided by love, humility, and moral purpose, society becomes stronger and more united.

Why This Matters

Radical individualism matters because it influences many messages you hear today. You may hear messages that suggest that the most important thing in life is to follow your feelings, focus only on yourself, and avoid responsibilities that require sacrifice. Social media and entertainment often celebrate independence without the responsibility that should come with it. These ideas can make people forget that real happiness often comes from serving others, building strong families, and keeping commitments.

This also matters because your generation will help shape the future of your communities. When many people choose personal desire over responsibility, families and neighborhoods can weaken. When that happens, government often grows larger and personal freedom may shrink. Understanding radical individualism helps you see why the American founders emphasized virtue and why the gospel teaches service and the importance of covenants. True happiness comes from balancing personal choices with love and responsibility. Choosing to care for others and honor your commitments helps preserve the freedom and stability that bless your life today.

Conclusion

Your Role in Preserving Freedom

The story of America is the story of a people who believed that freedom is a sacred gift from God and that every person has divine worth. The founders created a nation built on the idea that rights come from God, not from rulers, and that government exists to protect those rights. They studied history, sought to understand human nature, and designed a system that could preserve liberty through responsibility, virtue, and wise self-government.

Throughout this book, you have learned how the American founding grew from centuries of ideas about justice, natural law, and human dignity. You saw how documents such as the Declaration of Independence, the Constitution, the Bill of Rights, and the Federalist Papers helped shape a new nation based on agency, accountability, and limited government. These documents remind us that freedom requires structure, balance, and a clear understanding of right and wrong.

You also learned how the three branches of government work together to help protect liberty. The legislative branch makes laws, the executive branch carries them out, and the judicial branch interprets them. Each branch has its own limits and responsibilities so that no single person or group becomes too powerful. This system reflects the founders' belief that human beings can do great good but can also make harmful choices at times. Dividing power protects freedom for everyone.

The chapters on political parties, systems of government, and methods of control helped you see how different ideas influence daily life. Some systems encourage virtue, opportunity, and moral responsibility, while others can lead to instability or too much control. Understanding these differences can help you recognize ideas that protect liberty and ideas that threaten it.

You also studied modern ideologies that shape today's culture. These ideas influence how people think about truth, family, identity, responsibility, and government. Some strengthen the moral foundations that support freedom. Others weaken those foundations by separating freedom from accountability or by encouraging people to look to government instead of family, faith, or community. Knowing these ideas can help you stay grounded in truth while respecting others and showing compassion to those who see the world differently.

Across every chapter, one message has been clear. *Freedom survives best when individuals choose to live with virtue, self-control, courage, and love.* Strong families, honest communities, and moral citizens often do more to protect liberty than any law or policy. When people use their agency to bless others and strengthen their homes, society becomes safer, happier, and more stable.

The restored gospel gives this message deeper and eternal meaning. God created His children to learn, to choose, to grow, and to become more like Him. Agency is central to His plan of happiness for us. The principles that protect freedom also protect your ability to live the gospel, serve others, and prepare for eternal life. When we use our freedom with gratitude and righteousness, we honor the gifts God has given us.

As you go forward, try to remember what you have learned. Strive to be a responsible citizen. Stay informed. Keep your commitments. Value truth. Strengthen your family. Show respect to others, even when you disagree. Defend the freedoms that bless this nation. And above all, live in a way that honors God, who gave you your agency and who desires your happiness.

Liberty is a blessing. It requires protection and it invites us to rise to our highest potential. By choosing virtue, wisdom, and faith, you can help preserve freedom for yourself, your family, and future generations.

www.ingramcontent.com/pod-product-compliance
Lightning Source LLC
LaVergne TN
LVHW020653100826
845148LV00012B/2471

* 9 7 8 0 9 4 1 8 4 6 4 5 5 *